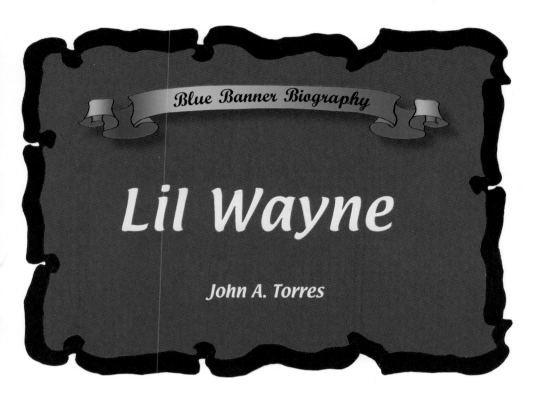

Blue Banner Biography

Lil Wayne

John A. Torres

Mitchell Lane
PUBLISHERS

P.O. Box 196
Hockessin, Delaware 19707
Visit us on the web: www.mitchelllane.com
Comments? email us: mitchelllane@mitchelllane.com

Mitchell Lane
PUBLISHERS

Printing   1   2   3   4   5   6   7   8   9

Blue Banner Biographies

Akon	Alan Jackson	Alicia Keys
Allen Iverson	Ashanti	Ashlee Simpson
Ashton Kutcher	Avril Lavigne	Bernie Mac
Beyoncé	Bow Wow	Brett Favre
Britney Spears	Carrie Underwood	Chris Brown
Chris Daughtry	Christina Aguilera	Christopher Paul Curtis
Ciara	Clay Aiken	Cole Hamels
Condoleezza Rice	Corbin Bleu	Daniel Radcliffe
David Ortiz	Derek Jeter	Eminem
Eve	Fergie (Stacy Ferguson)	50 Cent
Gwen Stefani	Ice Cube	Jamie Foxx
Ja Rule	Jay-Z	Joe Flacco
Jennifer Lopez	Jessica Simpson	J. K. Rowling
John Legend	Johnny Depp	JoJo
Justin Berfield	Justin Timberlake	Kanye West
Kate Hudson	Keith Urban	Kelly Clarkson
Kenny Chesney	Kristen Stewart	Lance Armstrong
Leona Lewis	**Lil Wayne**	Lindsay Lohan
Mariah Carey	Mario	Mary J. Blige
Mary-Kate and Ashley Olsen	Miguel Tejada	Missy Elliott
Nancy Pelosi	Natasha Bedingfield	Nelly
Orlando Bloom	P. Diddy	Paris Hilton
Peyton Manning	Pink	Queen Latifah
Rihanna	Ron Howard	Rudy Giuliani
Sally Field	Sean Kingston	Selena
Shakira	Shontelle Layne	Soulja Boy Tell 'Em
Taylor Swift	T.I.	Timbaland
Tim McGraw	Toby Keith	Usher
Vanessa Anne Hudgens	Zac Efron	

Library of Congress Cataloging-in-Publication Data
Torres, John Albert.
 Lil Wayne / by John A. Torres.
     p. cm. — (Blue banner biographies)
 Includes bibliographical references and index.
 ISBN 978-1-58415-768-7 (library bound)
 1. Lil Wayne—Juvenile literature. 2. Rap musicians—United States—Biography—Juvenile literature.
I. Title.
 ML3930.L49T67 2009
 782.421649092—dc22
 [B]
                                                                                    2009006307

PARENTS AND TEACHERS STRONGLY CAUTIONED:
The Story of Lil Wayne's life may not be appropriate for younger readers.

ABOUT THE AUTHOR: John A. Torres is an award-winning newspaper journalist for *Florida Today*. Based on the Florida coast, he has reported from Indonesia, Mexico, Haiti, Italy, and other places around the world. He is the author of more than 40 books, including *Timbaland*, *Usher*, and *P. Diddy* for Mitchell Lane Publishers. A big music fan, Torres was hyped to pen this book about rap music's hottest superstar, Lil Wayne.

PUBLISHER'S NOTE: The following story has been thoroughly researched, and to the best of our knowledge represents a true story. While every possible effort has been made to ensure accuracy, the publisher will not assume liability for damages caused by inaccuracies in the data and makes no warranty on the accuracy of the information contained herein. This story has not been authorized or endorsed by Lil Wayne.

Blue Banner Biography

Lil Wayne, who claims he is from another planet, takes flight during the 2008 Powerhouse Concert. He has earned his reputation as one of the hardest working artists in the music business.

Extraterrestrial Talent

*I*t should have been a morning of celebration and relaxation. Rap superstar Lil Wayne had just received a phone call from his longtime friend and manager Cortez Bryant, who had great news. Lil Wayne's latest CD, *Tha Carter III*, had just sold a million copies in only one week.

No one, not even the most confident music industry executives, expected that—especially in 2008, when the U.S. economy was in a recession. Not only were a million copies sold, but there was Lil Wayne—dreadlocks, tattoos of tears coming down his face, and his smooth, soulful rapping voice—already at the number one spot on the Billboard singles chart with his smash hit "Lollipop."

Did Lil Wayne allow himself to rest or celebrate? No way. Instead he spent that morning recording a brand-new song about the record sales called "A Milli." He rapped:

A million sold, first day I went gold,
How do I celebrate? Work on *Tha Carter IV*.

A lot of people—Lil Wayne included—consider him to be the greatest rapper of all time. While that is still up for debate, one thing is not: Lil Wayne has to be the hardest working man in the music business. After all, some reports say the New Orleans native recorded more than 1,000 songs over a two-year period, starting in 2006. While the number is staggering, the twenty-six-year-old rapper makes the creativity sound like a train he is unable to stop.

> "I gotta keep on going because I still don't have the crown . . . That tells me I'm not going hard enough. That tells me I've done something wrong."

"It's a faucet I can't turn off," he said from a Miami recording studio, where he was known to work until the sunrise on new recordings. "I can try and ignore it but I can never turn it off. And I gotta keep on going because I still don't have the crown. Someone else just won the Best Male Hip-Hop Artist at the BET Awards. Why not me? Huh? That tells me I'm not going hard enough. That tells me I've done something wrong."

His fans would argue against him on that point. For hip-hop and rap fans alike, Lil Wayne has done nothing but create great music for them to listen and dance to, and lots of it. So much, in fact, that some people at his record label—Universal Motown—were worried that Lil Wayne was putting too much music out and that he was appearing on too many people's records.

In 2007 alone, Lil Wayne made more than $2 million just by collaborating on other people's songs. That does not include the massive amount of music that made its way onto

Lil Wayne loves to record and perform, though sometimes his record label worries he is doing too much.

the airwaves through blogs, ringtones, Internet sites, and unofficial releases.

The executives were afraid that fans would not buy the CDs since there was already so much of his music available. They tried telling Lil Wayne to slow down, but he responded by telling them it was impossible. He said asking him to rap less would be like telling him to breathe less.

> Executives tried telling Lil Wayne to slow down, but . . . he said asking him to rap less would be like telling him to breathe less.

Lil Wayne, who was born Dwayne Michael Carter Jr., admits that he is simply addicted to recording music. In fact, he doesn't even write down lyrics or melodies as they pop into his head. He travels everywhere with a mini-recorder hooked up to his portable hard drive, and he simply records the raps as they come. He's bragged that he can write five songs a day with that method.

If you talk to Lil Wayne long enough, or read the things he says, you'll know he has an explanation for his success, the label of greatest rapper in the world that he places on himself, and the amount of music he is able to record. Lil Wayne sometimes claims to be from another planet. The funny thing is, no one is sure whether he is joking or if he really believes it.

"I'm a Martian, yes, and if you understand any of this then you're [God]," he says with a laugh. On his song "Phone Home," Lil Wayne says: "We are not the same, I am a Martian."

The 5-foot, 6-inch-tall Lil Wayne, who calls himself Weezy, performs onstage with T-Pain in 2008. Lil Wayne doesn't mind appearing in a supporting role, whether onstage or on a recording.

While he may not be from another planet, Lil Wayne has traveled a great distance from a troubled childhood that included drugs and guns in one of the country's toughest neighborhoods. He has become a man on the roll of his life who seems to be able to play whatever his fans are craving to hear. And if he comes across as a braggart or someone who thinks he knows it all, it's because in the music studio where he records his raps, he definitely knows a lot.

"I love the studio," he says. "It feels like going into a classroom, you know you didn't study everything, the test gets in front of you, and you're like, I know all the answers. That's how I feel when I get into the studio, like I know all the answers."

CHAPTER 2

A Kid With Attitude

L il Wayne comes across as a thug, a streetwise gangster with no education. In some respects, that is just an image that the record companies and music industry executives want the public to believe. Lil Wayne's story and the things that shaped who he is happen to be a lot more complex than the stereotypical "gangsta" background. In fact, Lil Wayne was accepted to college.

Lil Wayne was born on September 27, 1982, in the tough Holly Grove area of New Orleans, Louisiana — the murder capital of the United States. The troubled 17th Ward of New Orleans stretches from the Mississippi River to Lake Pontchartrain.

Parts of New Orleans are so tough that people will not even phone for help when they hear gunfire. In the summer of 2005, a local university conducted an experiment one afternoon. They had police fire 700 blank bullet rounds throughout a New Orleans neighborhood. No one — not one single person — called police. New Orleans has long been known as a city where people are either afraid of going to the

Lil Wayne shows off the fruits of his labor — a diamond-encrusted grill.

police for help or they would rather take care of problems in their own way.

Lil Wayne grew up in a small apartment with his mother, Jacida Carter, who worked as a chef. He barely knew his father, Dwayne Michael Turner, who had no part in raising him.

Lil Wayne's childhood room was very plain — but that was the way he liked it. There were no posters, the walls were painted off-white, and there was barely a toy in sight. In fact, Lil Wayne says he never played with an action figure. He had a calendar on one wall, and there was a television set with a Nintendo video game system.

The pride of his room, the centerpiece, was bunk beds. Even though he was an only child, Lil Wayne asked his mother if he could have bunk beds because he earned such high grades in school. "I did perfect at school," he says. "So, at home I was king."

Lil Wayne does not talk much about his childhood, but he was such a good student that he was admitted to the gifted student program at Lafayette Elementary School. Even though books and homework were the first priority, by the age of eight years old, Lil Wayne started coming up with his own raps. He would rap all throughout the house for his mother. It wasn't long before he started rapping on his front porch in front of neighbors. He even started his own rap crew of little kids like himself. They called themselves K.W.A. — Kids With Attitude.

> *It wasn't long before he started rapping on his front porch in front of neighbors. He even started his own rap crew of little kids like himself.*

"Neighborhood girls would be in the audience," he says, laughing about his interest in girls at such a young age.

When he got to middle school, Lil Wayne had grown from the front porch performances and wanted to do more. He joined the drama club at Eleanor McMain Secondary School, and landed the big role of the Tin Man in the school's performance of *The Wiz*.

He continued getting good grades, but the seedy toughness of the neighborhood started to creep into his life. Lil Wayne's mother got involved with a drug dealer. Lil Wayne found one of her boyfriend's guns and started carrying it to school. He would get straight As in class and then show the gun to his friends. It was almost as if Lil Wayne could split himself into two different and distinct people.

"At school he could be as brainy as he wanted to be," said Cortez Bryant. "But when the bell rang, he was back out in the jungle."

In fact, the neighborhood was so crazy that his own mother bought him a gun only two years later. Lil Wayne says that his mother told him to shoot and kill anyone who threatened to hurt him. That may sound shocking to some, but that is not unusual in high-crime urban areas.

What may even be more shocking is that Lil Wayne nearly killed himself accidentally with another gun in the home. He was home alone when he came across a .44 handgun that belonged to his mother's boyfriend. Lil Wayne started posing with the gun in front of a mirror. He was listening to rap music and waving the gun more and more as he was imitating Biggie Smalls. His finger slipped on the triger and he pulled it back, sending a bullet right into his chest. The bullet missed his heart by only two inches.

> *"At school he could be as brainy as he wanted to be," said Cortez Bryant. "But when the bell rang, he was back out in the jungle."*

"It was like a chopper hit me," Lil Wayne says. "But the bullet went straight through, and I bounced back in two weeks." In fact, it was two weeks before he was taken off life support; his recovery took much longer. But Lil Wayne is not one to dwell on the past.

Lil Wayne takes in a Nets-Heat play-off game in 2006 with Birdman. He has never forgotten his New Orleans roots and the people who helped him rise to the top. Lil Wayne and Birdman have been friends since Wayne was a child.

Hot Boy

During this time, the years just before becoming a teenager, Lil Wayne made friends with Bryan "Baby" Williams, a New Orleans rapper and the owner of Cash Money Records. Williams, who was also known by his stage name Birdman, was older than Lil Wayne and became a mentor of sorts to him. Constantly trying to impress his new friend, Lil Wayne woud leave freestyle raps on Williams's answering machine.

Lil Wayne was branching out from the local rap scene. He and his friends started going around the neighborhoods of Holly Grove and Dixon and "battle rapping."

Battle rapping is when two or more rappers try to insult or "diss" each other through the use of clever lyrics that are improvised on the spot. The entire battle is done without scripted, or written down, lyrics. The idea is to convince anyone watching that you are the better rapper.

Lil Wayne was earning a reputation as a good improviser of freestyle lyrics. He started doing less at school and more at Cash Money Records, where he was paid to run errands.

Pretty soon Williams signed Lil Wayne to a contract and started using him on some Cash Money–distributed songs.

At the age of fourteen, Lil Wayne quit school and became a professional rapper. Even though Lil Wayne was an honor student at Marion Abramson Senior High School, his mother encouraged him to quit.

> **Gone was the scholar, the kid who got great grades in school. The only person left was a streetwise rapper.**

"My momma graduated from high school while she was pregnant with me," Lil Wayne says. "Maybe that's why she didn't care for me to graduate from high school. My momma made me drop out of the tenth grade. She came walking past my room one morning and saw me putting my pistol in my backpack."

She flipped out and couldn't believe that he needed to take a gun with him to school. Were the schools that unsafe? she asked. He never went back. Later on, Lil Wayne would say that once he went on tour as a rapper, he came back as a different person. Gone was the scholar, the kid who got great grades in school. The only person left was a streetwise rapper.

In 1993, Lil Wayne and fellow rapper and friend B.G. joined forces and called themeselves the B.G.s. They released a record that was a mild success locally called *True Stories*.

A year later, Lil Wayne became the youngest member of one of the first superstar boy groups around. The Hot Boys, or Hot Boy$, as they were sometimes called, started recording music for Cash Money Records. The group

Lil Wayne flashes his arm tattoos while he and the other members of the group Juvenile and the Hot Boys sport the Cash Money bling. The band was honored at the 1999 Source Hip-Hop Awards.

consisted of the hottest rappers already signed to the label: Lil Wayne, Juvenile, Turk, and B.G.

The group became an instant success with their first album, *Get It How U Live!* Then in 1999 the band broke through with *Guerrilla Warfare*, which reached number one on the Billboard Top R&B/Hip-Hop Albums Chart.

The band is still well known, and there has been talk of a reunion. They are best remembered for helping Lil Wayne cut his teeth musically and also for the songs "We On Fire" and "I Need a Hot Girl."

Guerrilla Warfare caused a lot of people and music fans to take notice of this young talent who called himself Lil Wayne. There was some hope that maybe one day he would branch out and have a successful rap career on his own. They had no idea that one day he would boast he was "the greatest rapper in the world."

Known for spectacular showmanship and his croaking rhythmic rhymes, Lil Wayne gets close to the special effects blaze onstage in 2009.

CHAPTER 4

Tha Block Is Hot

Years of rap battles, freestyling, front porch concerts, and a stint with the Hot Boys had not only prepared Lil Wayne for a spectacular career as a rap superstar, but they also taught him to use his voice in a certain way. Music listeners always know a Lil Wayne song when they hear it. It's because his voice is . . . well, it's different. It's not silky smooth like Snoop Dogg's or twangy like Jay-Z's. Instead, it is a mix of gruffness and hoarseness that at the same time can sound very smooth and free-flowing. *Rolling Stone* described his voice as "a needling, grizzled croak that's one of the most distinctive sounds in pop music."

While he achieved notoriety singing and rapping with the Hot Boys, Lil Wayne also proved that he did not really need to be in a group to be popular. In 1999, at the age of seventeen, he released his first solo album, *Tha Block Is Hot*. The recording had a smash hit single of the same name, which VH1 named as one of the top 50 rap songs of all time.

The album achieved double platinum status—meaning it sold at least 2 million copies. It seemed that Lil Wayne had arrived, and he would certainly be music's next superstar.

The Source magazine nominated him for its Best New Artist award.

But superstardom did not come quickly. In 2000, Lil Wayne released his second solo disc, *Lights Out.* Critics were not impressed. They felt the lyrics or rhymes were not very clever or mature. The disc also was not promoted the way his first solo album was. The album failed to sell a million copies and was not considered a success.

> **Needing to reinvent himself, he did what he knows best. He started recording a lot of music and performing on other people's albums.**

There was a lot of pressure on Lil Wayne to use his next recording to elevate him back to stardom. Released in 2002, that recording, *500 Degreez,* failed to live up to the hype. The album was a hard-core collection of gangster and street crime imagery. Like many of Lil Wayne's songs, there was a lot of humor thrown in — but the fans didn't seem to get it.

Lil Wayne was in need of a giant hit. Needing to reinvent himself, he did what he knows best. He started recording a lot of music and performing on other people's albums. He worked hard to reestablish himself with his fans, even if it wasn't with a new album. In fact, fans would have to wait two years for his next official release.

To his credit, Lil Wayne realized that success does not come easy. It would take hard work, the same kind of dedication needed to be a star in other fields. In fact, he said it was sort of like being a sports star: "It takes practice, endurance, strength, style, speed, accuracy and all that," he said. "This is what makes us better at what we do in the music. Just like players in the NFL or the NBA who are the best. They are professionals and their sport is their life. . . . There is no such thing as an off-season for them."

When Lil Wayne is not in the recording studio or on stage, he is busy doing something that does not get a lot of attention: giving back. Lil Wayne often becomes Dwayne Michael Carter again for a day to go and speak with students at his old schools or others in the downtrodden New Orleans area. He is also heavily involved in the One Family Foundation—a nonprofit organization that helps children achieve their potential.

When he speaks at schools or with kids, Lil Wayne never pretends to be perfect. He has had problems with the law regarding drugs and guns, including an arrest in 2007 for felony gun possession, and several arrests for drug possession. He tells the students never to give up.

On January 12, 2009, Lil Wayne presented a check for $200,000 to help restore Harrell Park in New Orleans, a park for kids that had been destroyed by Hurricane Katrina. "The word today and the word forever is 'kids,' " he said.

> *When Lil Wayne is not in the recording studio or on stage, he is busy doing something that does not get a lot of attention: giving back.*

CHAPTER 5

"The Best Rapper Alive"

*I*n 2004, Lil Wayne lived up to his promise with the release of the outstanding album *Tha Carter*, a reference to himself. The lyrics and rhymes on this disc were much sharper, wittier, and explosive than on his previous two attempts.

He seemed to also regain his confidence. In fact, it was the first time that he referred to himself as "the best rapper alive," on a track called "Bring It Back."

In the song, Lil Wayne says he is "the best rapper alive since the best rapper retired." This is a reference to fellow rap superstar Jay-Z, who retired for a short period in 2003.

Also in 2004, Lil Wayne earned his General Educational Development Diploma (GED). He also married his high school sweetheart, Antonia "Toya" Johnson. They have a daughter together named Reginae. The marriage did not last, however, and the couple divorced in 2006. Not content with just a high school equivalency diploma, Lil Wayne later enrolled in online classes at the University of Houston.

While the album was a smash hit and did indeed propel Lil Wayne to the top of the rap kingdom, it was his

A special date for a special night: Lil Wayne took in the 51st Grammy Awards ceremony with his daughter Reginae in 2009. The New Orleans rapper was nominated for eight of the prestigious awards.

contributions to the song "Soldier" with Destiny's Child that earned him his first major critical acclaim. Released at the end of 2004, it marked the first time that mainstream pop music fans heard Lil Wayne working his rhymes. The collaboration earned him and Destiny's Child a Grammy Award nomination.

As is his trademark, Lil Wayne did not stop to enjoy his newfound success. He went right back into the music studio to start working on *Tha Carter II*. Released in 2005, this follow-up to *Tha Carter* sold 1.8 million records.

Once again on the recording, Lil Wayne boasts about being the best rapper alive. But in interviews he also talks about the work he puts into his success. He believes that nothing comes without hard work.

"As a man you're not supposed to expect a thing," he said. "I never expect nothing. You take care of right now and see how long you can stretch right now. If I'm focused on now then I'm alright."

> **What Lil Wayne needed was a huge crossover hit to establish himself as not just a rapper but as a pop music superstar.**

During this period, there was also some good-natured ribbing between Jay-Z—considered the greatest rapper ever by many—and the New Orleans rapper determined to take his crown. They exchanged songs in which they criticized each other and claimed the title for themselves.

Lil Wayne's next venture was to do an album with his mentor, friend, and longtime father figure, Bryan "Baby" Williams. The album, titled *Like Father, Like Son*, sold 750,000 copies.

But even though *GQ Magazine* named Lil Wayne the Workaholic Man of the Year for 2007, it seemed as if there was little higher he could go in the rap world. What Lil Wayne needed was a huge crossover hit to establish himself as not just a rapper but as a pop music superstar.

He would have to come up with a record that was softer than the gangsta-style rap he liked but still maintain the tough grit his fans had come to expect. That's what he sought to do when he started recording songs for *Tha Carter III*. The album was set to go when someone leaked some of the music onto the Internet. Radio deejays started playing the music.

The four biggest names in the rap music industry relax after performing at the 2009 Grammy Awards. From left to right are Kanye West, T.I., Jay-Z, and Lil Wayne. Each is known for his individual rap style.

This did not make Lil Wayne happy. He released that music as a small album called *The Leak*, and then went back to work on *Tha Carter III*.

His goal? To make an album that people would remember.

"It's one of those albums that people are waiting on, so I made it so that whatever is on it will stick to you," he told *Billboard* in 2008. "I'm taking my time with it. It's going to be a great album."

Tha Carter III hit record stores in June 2008. The lush arrangements, soulful rhymes, lyrical genius, and funky rhythms helped the disk sell more than a million copies after only one week. And with a hit crossover pop song

Lil Wayne flashes a proud, knowing smile as he hoists one of four Grammy Awards he took home in 2009. It was the biggest night in the young rapper's career.

"Lollipop," it appeared that Dwayne Michael Carter had at last achieved the moniker of "greatest rapper alive."

Of course, that wasn't official until his friend Jay-Z handed him the title during the song "Mr. Carter." Lil Wayne said he got misty-eyed when he heard what Jay-Z wrote for the song. "I share mike time with my heir," he raps. "Young Carter go farther, go further, go harder."

His hard work was rewarded with a classic album and an incredible eight Grammy Award nominations, including Album of the Year. He took home four: Best Rap Song ("Lollipop"), Best Rap Album (*Tha Carter III*), Best Rap Solo Performance ("A Milli"), and Best Rap Performance by a Duo or Group ("Swagga Like Us").

Lil Wayne appeared on the television show Total Request Live *in 2009. He hinted toward another Carter recording:* Tha Carter IV.

Lil Wayne, who has homes in Miami and Atlanta, is really only ever home when he is at a recording studio. In October 2008, he became a father for the second time, to a son named Dwayne Carter III. Details of the mother and boy's private life remain just that — private.

Lil Wayne has come of age and taken the title of greatest rapper. With his incredible work ethic and determination, it's a title he is sure to hold for quite some time. While he is not about to give it up anytime soon, and while he has hinted at doing *Tha Carter IV,* he told *Rolling Stone* in early 2009 that his next album, *Rebirth,* would be his first foray into rock music. Why the change? He called it a natural progression, and said, "I don't want to be the best rapper in the world. Not now. . . . I want to be the best. Period."

1982 Dwayne Michael Carter, aka Lil Wayne, is born on September 27 in New Orleans.

1990 He starts rapping at the age of eight.

1994 He accidentally shoots himself in the chest while playing with a gun.

1996 He quits school at age fourteen to become a professional rapper.

1997 He releases the album *Get It How U Live!* with the group the Hot Boys.

1999 The group releases the album *Guerrilla Warfare*. Lil Wayne releases his first solo album, *Tha Block Is Hot*.

2000 He releases his second solo album, *Lights Out*.

2002 He releases *500 Degreez*.

2004 He marries Toya Johnson, the mother of his daughter Reginae, on February 14 and earns his General Educational Development Diploma (GED). He releases the smash album *Tha Carter*.

2005 He follows it up with *Tha Carter II*. He enrolls in the University of Houston to study political science, taking courses online.

2006 He and Toya divorce. He releases *Like Father, Like Son*, with Birdman, aka Baby.

2007 He is arrested in New York and charged with felony gun possession.

2008 He releases the smash hit *Tha Carter III* and begins working on *Tha Carter IV*. His son, Dwayne Carter III, is born on October 22.

2009 He is arrested in Yuma, Arizona, in January and charged with three counts of drug possession. He wins four Grammy Awards. In March, he stands trial for a 2006 arrest in Atlanta for drug possession; the judge rules that the search was illegal and he is exonerated. After delays to clear copyright issues on some of his samples, his rock album *Rebirth* is scheduled for a summer release. *Tha Carter IV* is slated to be released just a few months later.

DISCOGRAPHY

Albums

2009	*Rebirth*
2008	*Tha Carter III*
2007	*Da Drought 3* (mix tape)
	The Drought Is Over 2: The Carter III Sessions (mix tape)
	The Leak
2006	*Dedication 2* (mix tape)
	Like Father, Like Son
2005	*Tha Carter II*
2004	*Tha Carter*
2002	*500 Degreez*
2000	*Lights Out*
1999	*Tha Block Is Hot*

SELECTED AWARDS

2009	Grammy Awards: Best Rap Album (*Tha Carter III*); Best Rap Performance by a Duo or Group ("Swagga Like Us"); Best Rap Solo Performance ("A Milli"); Best Rap Song ("Lollipop")
2008	BET Award: Viewers' Choice
	MTV Music Award: Best Hip-Hop Video
2007	BET Awards: Viewers' Choice; Best Hip-Hop Artist Ozone Awards: Best Male Rap Artist; Best Lyricist; Mixtape Monster; Best Video ("We Takin' Over")
	Vibe Awards: Hip-Hop Artist of the Year; Best Mixtape of the Year; Best Collaboration

Books

If you enjoyed this book about Lil Wayne, you might also enjoy the following Blue Banner Biographies from Mitchell Lane Publishers:

50 Cent
Akon
Ja Rule
Jay-Z
John Legend

Kanye West
P. Diddy
Sean Kingston
Soulja Boy Tell 'Em
T.I.

Works Consulted

Binelli, Mark. "Life on Planet Wayne." *Rolling Stone*, April 16, 2007.

Checkoway, Laura. "The Art of Storytelling." *Vibe*, November 2007.

Concepcion, Mariel. "Lil Wayne: Smoke and Mirrors." *Billboard*, February 9, 2008, p. 40.

Ex, Kris. "American Psycho." *Complex*, January 2008, p. 54.

Gordon, Allen. "Lil Wayne." *Murder Dog*, August 2007, p. 82.

Hoard, Christian. "Lil Wayne." *Rolling Stone*, May 1, 2008, p. 60.
    http://www.rollingstone.com/artists/lilwayne/articles/
    story/20274122/best_mc_lil_wayne

Jyle. "Lil Wayne Donate's $200,000 for New Park." January 13, 2009.
    http://www.hiphoproll.com/lil-wayne-donates-200000-for-
    new-park/

"Lil Wayne—Cameras Banned in Lil Wayne Trial," *Contact Music*, May 12, 2009.
    http://www.contactmusic.com/news.nsf/article/
    cameras%20banned%20in%20lil%20wayne%20trial_1103155

Meadows-Ingram, Benjamin. "Touch the Sky." *Vibe*, May 2008, p. 84.

FURTHER READING

"New Orleans Murder Rate on the Rise Again; Homicide Rate Nowhere Near '94 Peak but Still 10 Times National Average." MSNBC, August 18, 2005, http://www.msnbc.msn.com/id/8999837/

Thomas, Datwon. "Lil Wayne: Space Oddity." *XXL Magazine*, October 2008, p. 80.

Weiner, Jonah. "Lil Wayne: There Is None Higher." *Blender*, September 2008, p. 53.

Web Addresses
Official Lil Wayne Website
www.lilwayne_online.com
Official Lil Wayne MySpace Page
www.myspace.com/lilwayne
One Family Foundation
http://www.1familyfoundation.org/about.html
Universal Motown: Lil Wayne's Page
http://www.universalmotown.com/discography/artist/default.aspx?aid=433

INDEX